A CELTIC WAY

floral designs

REVEREND MAC

This book is one of a special limited edition

A CELTIC WAY

floral designs

REVEREND WILLIAM McMILLAN

SPIRIT OF THE ROSE

Foreword

Shane Connolly
Floral Designer and Author.
Florist By Appointment to
HRH the Prince of Wales.

When Oscar Wilde declared, " I have put my genius into my life, all that I have put into my works is my talent," he might well, in an odd way, have been describing the subject of this book, the Reverend McMillan. The Reverend, however, being of a more genuinely modest disposition than Mr Wilde, would never dream of saying such a thing about himself.

His unique talent with flowers is self-evident, both in the exquisite images that follow and to anyone lucky enough to have seen his work, or attended one of his unforgettable demonstrations, but it is the extraordinary life-enhancing person behind the artist that this book really celebrates. It is a celebration that is both an agony and an anathema to the modest Mac.

I had heard of the Reverend long before I met him - his reputation most definitely preceded him. Rarely though has expectation been so far surpassed by reality, and my admiration and respect, both as a fellow Celt and fellow flower arranger, knew no bounds.

It is the unadulterated agreeableness of the man that is the real abiding memory; the wonderful un-malicious wit, (often directed at himself) the charm, the unfeigned interest in people, the kindness and generosity with time and talent and that phenomenal energy - often in spite of a body that stubbornly refuses to adjust to any time zone outside of Northern Ireland.

Unsurprisingly, the Reverend Mac has put his talent to thoroughly selfless good use over the years and has deservedly been lauded and applauded by the great and the good: an MBE in recognition of the enormous sums of money he has raised for charity; the Albert Schweitzer Award for promoting religious freedom in Northern Ireland; and the highest honours and awards possible from the National Association of Flower Arranging Societies of Great Britain and the Garden Clubs of America.

What is surprising is that he remains so sincerely unassuming and unpretentious, the achievements neither flaunted nor overrated. In the flighty world of flower design, these traits are rare even in the less accomplished. Rarer still is the combination of his serious encyclopaedic knowledge of plants and childlike enthusiasm and joy in using them in his designs.

The Reverend Mac is a man who has indeed put his genius into life and living. He is a true inspiration. It is a pleasure to know him and an honour to introduce this book, where his joy of life and love of flowers glint from every page.

5

floral designs A CELTIC WAY
The Very Reverend William McMillan, MBE,MA,ML (GCA)

To my wife Sheila and the members of my family, who reluctantly agreed that I should attempt another book, I dedicate this publication with love.

It was the mesmerising, artistic enthusiasm of Miss Julia Clements OBE, VMH, which encouraged me to take the first step of what was to become a fascinating journey through the world of flowers. I have been honoured by her friendship and inspired by her work. Julia, 101 years old, continues to encourage and cajole me to greater efforts. Words are inadequate to express my gratitude, but I hope that within these designs she will see her influence.

This book would not have been possible without the support of Eammon Kelly of Kelly Flowers International who generously sponsored all the imported plant and flower materials used. I am extremely grateful to him, his family and the members of his staff who were diligent in their efforts to supply me with 'the rare and the beautiful.'

David Lloyd's exceptional skill as a photographer and Annie Beagent's artistic flair in designing the layout of this publication deserve more than a mere 'thank you.' I was motivated by their enthusiasm and record my sincere gratitude. It has been an honour to work with David and Annie whose talents have been recognised by the awards they have received. David was named 'Photographer of the Year 2004' by The Garden Writers' Guild for a portfolio of images taken from their book, *Spirit of the Rose* and they both travelled to Japan recently after receiving an 'Award for Literary Excellence' from the World Federation of Rose Societies for the same publication.

Audrey and David Balderstone arranged the numerous necessary visits to England, offering me wonderful hospitality and much needed advice. Audrey was a tireless helper, travelling from London to Belfast to assist with the designs. I could not have completed all the arrangements in the time available without her help and that of Ian McNeil, Ann Traynor and Yolanda Campbell. To all of them I am indebted.

My good friend Father Sean McAvoy, with Patrick Kelly and Neil McNamee of Kelly Flowers International, willingly gave of their time to check that the plant identifications were correct. I thank them.

While visiting the Chelsea Flower Show I met many friends connected with the Barbados and Jamaican Horticultural Societies. They insisted on letting me have exotic materials they had used on their stands. Unfortunately I was not able to work quickly enough to include all their gifts, but I thank them for their thoughtfulness. Mrs Ann Ramsey of Jamaica was particularly generous in supplying a rare orchid, among other items.

Those who purchased my first book, *Beyond Mere Words*, and suggested another, are responsible for this second attempt. I hope it will justify their belief in my ability to create Floral Designs in a Celtic Way.

It is full summer now, the heart of June;
Not yet the sunburnt reapers are astir
Upon the upland meadow where too soon
Rich Autumn time, the season's usurer
Will lend his hoarded gold to all the trees,
And see his treasure scattered by the wild
and spendthrift breeze...

The Garden of Eros
Oscar Wilde

The silence during the meal was prolonged and tense. The young man tried desperately to encourage some communication between his glamorous young student friend and his mother, who was struggling to accept the idea of an English girl in her son's life. Then his father, with a wicked twinkle in his eye said, "Excuse me, but we must finish our meal quickly. The woman next door needs her plates back before six o'clock!"

A moment of horror, followed by peals of relieved laughter broke the ice and an evening of good Irish craic* followed.

Such was the genetic legacy of the Reverend William McMillan. From a mother who was a strict disciplinarian and a father with a great sense of humour Mac inherited a combination of qualities he has carried into all aspects of his life, be it within the church or in the world of floral art.

*lively Irish conversation

10

12

Born in the small Cathedral town of Dromore, Co. Down, Northern Ireland, Mac's early life centred around the Church and his maternal grandmother's garden. Here he was given an area to cultivate provided he kept it neat and tidy. His work was supervised by a grandmother who looked remarkably like Gertrude Jekyll and, like the great English gardener, she too had a wonderful sense of colour and texture which she attempted to instil in her young grandson.

He was not always biddable, however, and his boyhood antics resulted in a wise teacher predicting that he would end up either in the pulpit or on the stage. This followed an occasion when the family cat died and the bereaved William, at the tender age of six years, buried her in the local graveyard with solemn ritual, broken only by the outraged cries of his mother when she discovered that her best satin dress had been used as the shroud. His grandmother was equally horrified to learn that her finest roses had been cut to make the wreath!

Following seven years of University in England Mac returned to Northern Ireland to be ordained and installed to the charge of congregations in Newry and Warrenpoint in Co. Down.

He tells the story of his first encounter with one of his parishioners, a taciturn farmer. Desperately trying to make conversation Mac said; 'That was a very long lane up to your house." whereupon the farmer replied; "Aye, but sure, if it had been any shorter it wouldn't have reached the door." Here was the caustic Irish humour with which he felt very much at ease.

One of the perks, or some might say, pains, of living in a tied Manse in Ireland, is the vast garden. A century ago such acreage would have been used for vegetable growing as an essential addition to the minister's meagre income. To Mac it was a glorious blessing. Encouraged by his father, he began to develop a keen interest in plants, their history, habits, origins and how best to care for them.

Inspiration
Lady Seton (Julia Clements, OBE, VMH)

Photograph by Mike Pannett

As the minister, Mac appreciated the floral arrangements prepared in the church for weddings and special occasions. Nevertheless, at times he could not resist making a few alterations which he was sure 'improved' the designs.

It was while hunting for plants at a garden show that Mac wandered into a marquee where Julia Clements, the doyenne of flower arrangers, was demonstrating methods of arranging roses to their best advantage. Struck by the ease with which she appeared to create a so-called crescent arrangement, and a mass arrangement for a church, Mac's interest was captivated.

"I would love to be able to do that," he thought. He bought her book, *Floral Roundabout* and decided that from then on he would do the church flowers himself.

16

The interior of the 18th~Century Meeting House at The Glebe, Dunmurry where Mac has been the minister since 1970.

This Tiffany stained glass window, the only one in the meeting house, depicts the original garden.

Gaining experience in the school of trial and error Mac realised that while he had a 'flair' he had much to learn about this art form. By this time, 1964, he had married Sheila. With a busy parish, a wife and later four children to care for, there was not much opportunity to pursue this new interest in depth.

In 1970 Mac was appointed to the Dunmurry Church on the outskirts of Belfast and during an enforced convalescence, following an illness, he was introduced to a teacher of flower arranging who held classes in her home for groups of ladies. Reluctant to be the only male, he was put at ease when she agreed to teach two classes at the same time - the ladies in the dining room and Mac in the kitchen!

It was when he learned that many English and Continental designers were in fact men that Mac no longer felt the need to ask Sheila to pretend that she did the arrangements in the Manse. From then on he openly agreed to 'do the flowers' for all sorts of occasions.

Mac's hobby was becoming serious, but for his children, it was a hobby too far. It was bad enough having a Parson as a father but one who was also a flower arranger was too much. One morning, on seeing his dad dash around clutching some flowers and a swathe of material, one son was heard to muse; "Other boys' fathers go around the house with a spanner and a piece of wood, but what does ours do?"

All of his children, at one time or another, had to eat their words when they needed him to rustle up a Valentine token or decorate the church for a wedding. His oldest son is convinced that his job prospects were enhanced when the Chief Executive discovered him to be the son of the man about whom his wife raved after attending his flower arranging classes.

American potter Bruce Odell
frequently works in conjunction
with Angie Norris who developed the
technique of weaving pine needles
on to gourds. On this Raku pot she has
woven horse hair on to the lip of the
container. Once the pot had cooled
to 800 degrees, Bruce inserted coarse
strands of horse hair and feathers onto
the surface giving this pot its own
unique design.

25

Demands for club demonstrations had to be fitted into an already busy life and it was only through the support and encouragement of his long-suffering wife that Mac was able to keep both his parishioners and his flower arranging fans happy. Sheila was often heard to say that she encouraged him to travel because the only time she had some measure of peace and quiet was when he was away from home. His seemingly boundless energy allowed him to juggle work for the Church and the stage, but it could often be exhausting for those around him.

This was true for flower clubs in Jamaica where Mac's usual urge to work at great speed, without surrendering the discipline of meticulous workmanship, was noted. One observer of his hectic activity suggested that he should slow his pace in view of his increasing years. "Slow down man. You're in the waving gallery now!" he said. His family, however, always ready to keep Mac's feet on the ground, responded to the story with the comment that he is actually in the departure lounge!

28

Mac's zest for work has endeared him to his congregation and they are amazingly supportive of his 'hobby.' At the height of 'The Troubles' in Northern Ireland they encouraged him in his efforts to develop inter-religious and charitable work through the medium of floral art. Amused at the number of people who attended his flower arranging demonstrations he would often say;

"I cannot understand why so many of you are prepared to pay to see me on the stage when you could come and sit in the pews for free."

Persuaded and cajoled into taking his NAFAS (National Association of Flower Arranging Societies) National Demonstrator's test, Mac had to travel on the overnight ferry to attend the judging day in England. Never one to submit to rules and regulations, he nonetheless took the advice offered and soaked the oasis and attached it to his containers before setting out on his journey. Imagine his consternation the next morning when he discovered the oasis had frozen and there was no time to replace it.

Perhaps it was his "Irish blarney" and his instinctive way of dealing with any situation which persuaded the judges that he could be a worthy ambassador for NAFAS. He was launched onto the circuit. No-one noticed that he was colour blind!

Flower festivals soon followed, where Mac's interpretive skills, colour schemes, and use of space impressed the most hardened pragmatist and led to many years of designing similar events all over Ireland, England and abroad. His own Church members were delighted to have coaches full of people arriving to view spectacular designs and donate large amounts to charity in appreciation of what they had enjoyed.

Of course, in those early days, some were often wary of the strange and exotic blooms that Mac was having imported from all over the world. One parishioner was overheard to liken the first anthurium she saw to, "A scarlet woman with a cigarette hanging out of her mouth", while the Heliconia *veliger* "She-Kong", was said to resemble "a nest of dead rats".

On standing back to admire an ultra modern arrangement, Mac was rather deflated to hear one woman whisper to her friend, "I've seen better things thrown up on the end of a pitch-fork!"

33

A Flower Festival in the 18th Century Meeting House at The Glebe. Dunmurry

Mac's work is influenced by the sculptural form and his travels have provided an abundance of inspiration.

An enthusiastic friend from Co. Fermanagh has worn out several pairs of wellington boots, tramping through a secret private glen in all weathers, in search of Mac's requests for striking, multi-coloured moss and lichen-covered twigs. She was particularly busy after Mac responded to an invitation to decorate an area in the Crypt of Canterbury Cathedral, as part of a NAFAS Flower Festival "Christian Beginnings", staged to celebrate the arrival in England of St.Augustine. Working solely with moss and willow he created an ethereal, atmospheric tapestry across the ancient stone floor. Moss cloud trees and a specially commissioned piece of Irish sculpture movingly portrayed the title of his exhibit:

> 'The old order changeth, yielding place to new,
> And God fulfils Himself in many ways,
> Lest one good custom should corrupt the World'....

Morte d'Arthur
Alfred, Lord Tennyson

Many visitors wrote that they were moved to tears by the poignancy of the display.

Over the ensuing years Mac has encouraged moss to invade the Manse lawns and fields and has created a wild flower area. He is never happier than when making use of such materials even when the arrangement may be required for a sophisticated setting.

49

Mac finds it intriguing to use materials that few others would consider suitable for arrangements. It is not unusual to see a pile of turf and fir from the Irish bog-lands or a heap of earth-laden potatoes used to effect.

Never predictable but always inventive, when demonstrating Mac delights audiences with spectacular floral designs, poetry and tales of the mishaps that seem to befall him at every turn.

Mac made his mark at the World Show in Bath by incorporating sliced onions into the design. When the smell became too much, part of the arrangement had to be removed from the exhibition hall, much to his amusement and the disapproval of the judges.

On another occasion he was with a carpenter friend in the church graveyard surveying the damage to the building and its surrounds following a terrorist bombing on the railway track that ran alongside. The bemused expression on his friend's face was a study when Mac asked him to create a device that would fasten an old piece of stone onto a wooden base. The piece of stone was debris from one of the seventeenth century gravestones, flattened by the blast. The friend saw only a misshapen and battered stone. Mac saw the empty tomb on Easter Morning.

Similarly, in branches of cupressus accidentally sprayed with weed killer, Mac could see the poverty of the Nativity manger.

Preparing for his trip to the World Show in Toronto, where he was to be one of the International Demonstrators, Mac noticed a few strips of wood lying on the ground. They had short irregular cuts across them, left by the stone-cutter when he was shaping the sandstone blocks to repair the church wall. Instead of throwing them away, Mac gathered them up and took them with him. Three days later they became part of a "City Skyline" competition piece that won him "Best in Show".

Mac continues to be intrigued by the endless possibilities presented by unusual pieces of wood as is demonstrated in this design.

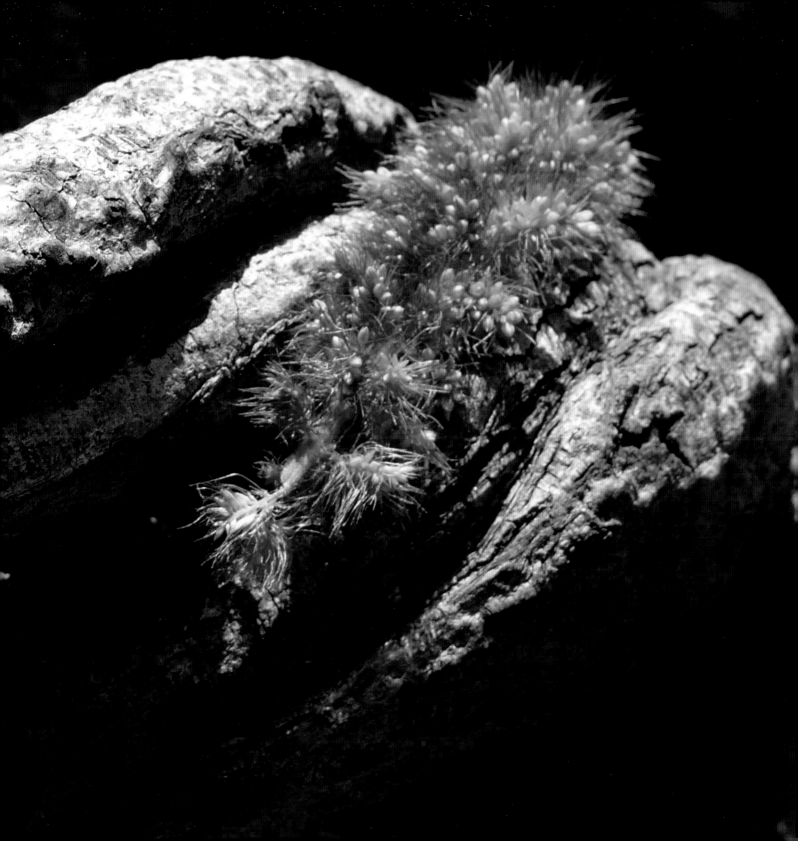

Celtic Twilight was the title chosen by Mac for his first National Demonstration for NAFAS at the Pavilion Theatre in Bournemouth in 1987. Haunting Celtic music and the use of Irish poetry created what Daphne Vagg in *The Flower Arranger* magazine called, "magical moments caught between fact and fantasy". The demonstration ended, Daphne observed, "in the dreamy colours of twilight and swirling mist. It was all part of the magic, which was greeted by applause of pop-star dimensions".

Although Mac had persuaded his two male helpers to wear Irish kilts for the demonstration, he kept to his usual dark suit, collar and tie. This is his traditional dress for demonstrating - even in the heat of Zimbabwe - and has been known to draw adverse comments from more colourful International Demonstrators!

Following the success of the demonstration in Bournemouth invitations poured in from all over the world. As a result, within a few years he was demonstrating or teaching not only throughout Europe but in Pakistan, Thailand, Japan, Australia, New Zealand, Zimbabwe, South Africa, Canada, North America, South America, Bermuda, and the Caribbean. These were exciting times and provided a welcome respite from the distressing political events that were happening in his own country at that time. Mac had sought to alleviate these, in part, by striving to bring together people from both sides of the religious and political divide through an interest in flower arranging.

Mac organised two of his most successful Festivals in the same city; one in the Roman Catholic Cathedral and the other in the Protestant Cathedral.

Travelling has provided Mac with wonderful opportunities to make new friends and to broaden his knowledge of plant material. His creative imagination is often tested to its limit on these visits, as he has to adapt his skills to work with unfamiliar and exotic materials at very short notice. He revels in these challenges and often returns home with a suitcase of intriguing mechanics, foliage and weird fruits instead of the shirts and trousers he set out with – much to the amazement of customs officials and the annoyance of his wife…

He has become a frequent visitor to America, demonstrating in museums which realise the appeal of the 'Art in Bloom' programmes. Museums in San Francisco, Boston, Salt Lake City, San Diego, New Orleans and numerous others attract large audiences for these week long events. They give him the opportunity to work with International Demonstrators and Professional Florists and to exchange ideas with them. Techniques learned at these events are usually incorporated into his own work and he is happy to acknowledge how much he owes to others.

On one memorable occasion an American demonstrator working with Mac was surprised to hear that he was a clergyman. Having earlier addressed him as "honey", he apologised and re-christened him, "Rev. Honey". Ron Morgan is one of America's most colourful teachers and demonstrators. From Ron, Mac acquired not only a new nickname, but also the art of using plant material which had been shaped by wrapping it around car tyres.

"We don't accomplish anything in this world alone...and whatever happens is the result of the whole tapestry of one's life and all the weavings of individual threads from one another that creates something."

Justice Sandra Day O'Connor
United States Supreme Court

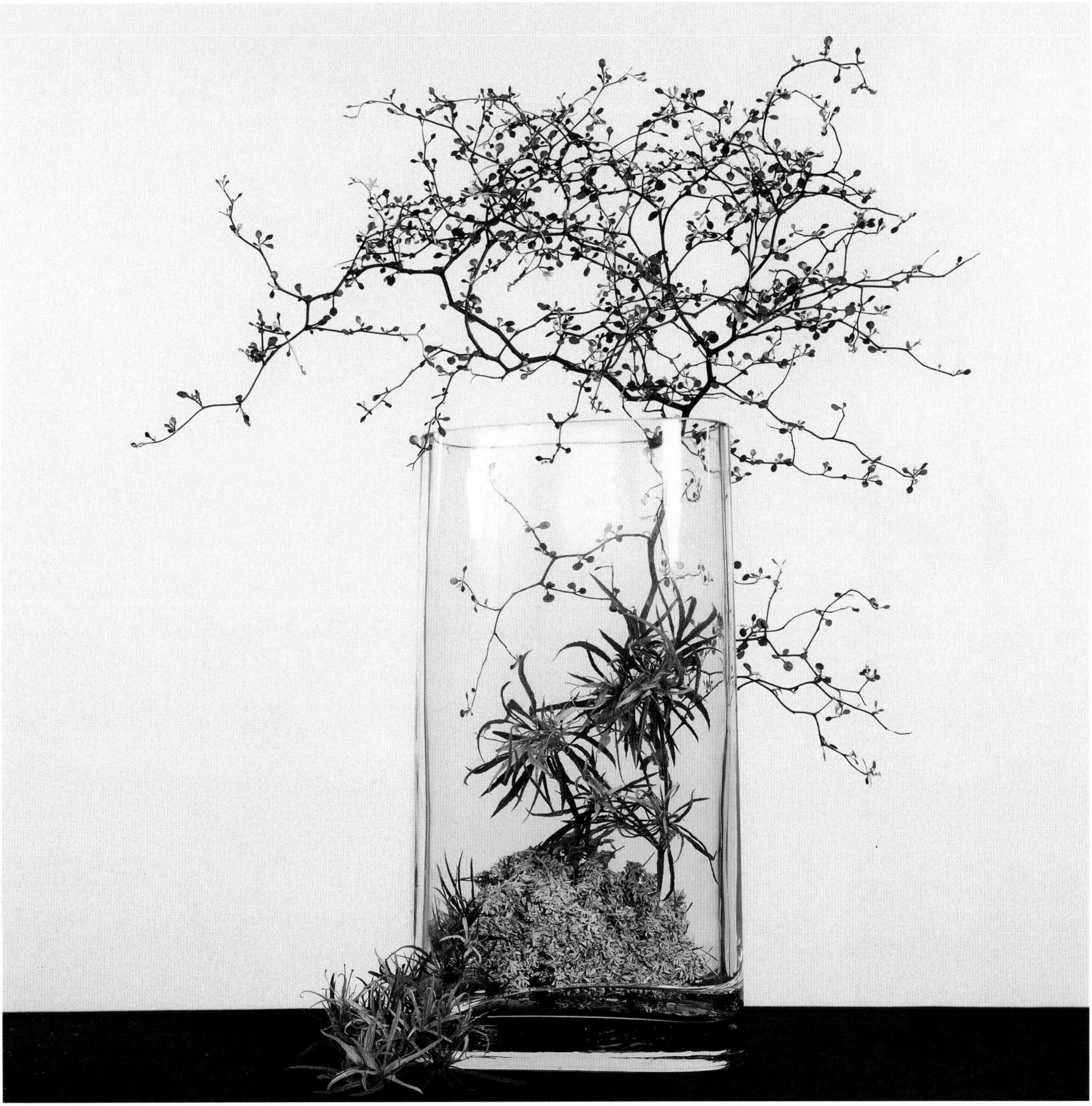

It was in San Francisco that Mac met a fellow Irishman, Shane Connolly. Through him he rediscovered the value of using flowers in season, arranged to striking effect without the usual mechanics.

He also learned a great deal from those who used colour to complement portraits and sculpture, together with the value of unusual pottery and ceramic containers. Containers were now to become more than just accessories and were used as an integral part when creating dramatic designs.

Always reluctant to encroach on the work of professional florists Mac rarely accepts wedding commissions. On one occasion just recently, however, he agreed to arrange the flowers for a special friend.

68

The designs in the hotel were demanding, using mainly one type of flower – Lily of the Valley. So-called 'waterfall' arrangements in specially commissioned tall glass vases took him and his helpers most of the night to create. Two guests, returning from breakfast, entered the ballroom. After admiring the flowers one asked, "Where did you do your training?" "I haven't had professional training" Mac replied. The lady turned to her friend, repeating the reply, whereupon the companion, with great seriousness said; "I do hope you don't mind me saying so, but I think that if you had a little bit of training you could go far." . . .

Containers of all shapes
and sizes inspire Mac.
This vibrant miniature
Royal Doulton vase is only
28cm tall and presented a
particular challenge, while
the broken container
opposite has acquired a
new lease of life.

73

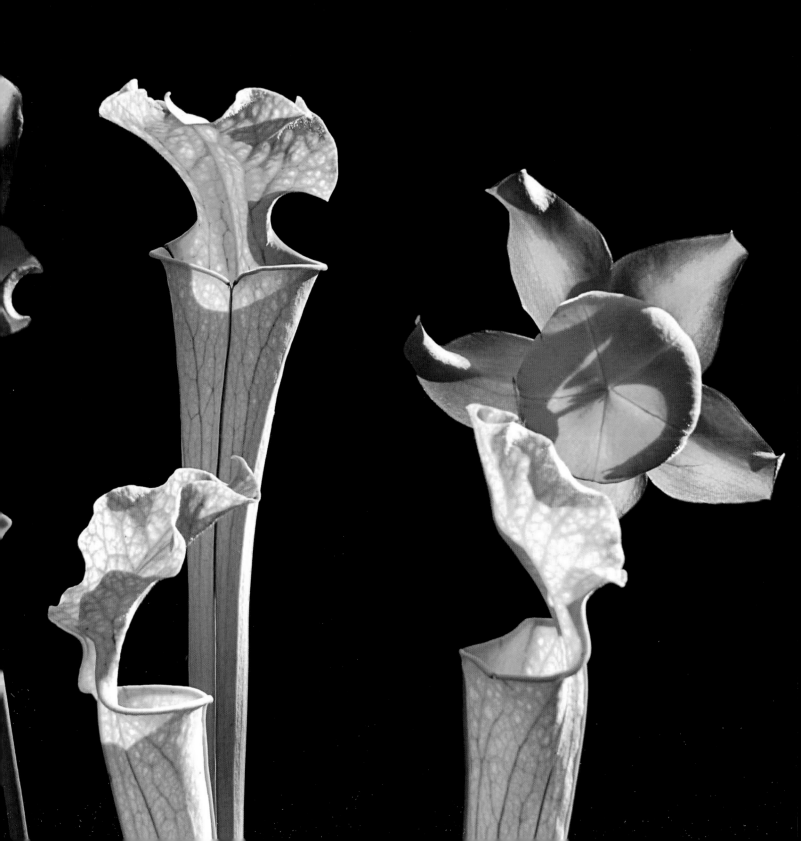

84

Photograph by Alastair McMillan

In more recent years, Mac has returned to his first love, transforming a two acre Manse field into a garden of wandering paths, streams and shrubs that are a tribute to Ireland's "forty shades of green". It is a flower arranger's garden, providing a cool, calm backdrop for his hectic lifestyle. Sheila helps out but has been banned from certain areas after uprooting some precious Irish seedlings, having mistaken them for weeds!

During his lectures and demonstrations Mac invariably reminds his audiences that many of the great gardeners and plant hunters have been, in fact, clergymen and missionaries.

Lecturing is another of Mac's talents and he loves to recount the stories of men and women of previous generations who travelled to unexplored lands, often risking life and limb, in search of rare and beautiful plants. Paying tribute to the zeal and determination of such people Mac creates designs which illustrate to the full the beauty of form and texture of plants we now mistakenly consider to be indigenous.

Photograph by Alastair McMillan

...to dream and gaze
And some Creator praise
For bounty that we nothing did to earn,
And rest content
With green beneath the leaves' translucent tent
In woods wherein the fern
Uncurls her crozier where the moss is wet
And the wild violet
Smokes blue along the pack-way in a haze.

He fashioned not the Lenten daffodil,
Nor set between the stones
Gentians by running water in the peat,
Nor sent the fleet
Of water- lilies sailing on the lake.

His art is imitation, and with love
On nature to improve,
The necessary fool has learnt to see
A better model, free
From labour, lavish in conceit, a wealth
Without a fence, ...since the woods more wise
Offer his eyes a garden at the foot of every tree.

The Garden. *Summer*
Vita Sackville-West

Top entrance to The Glebe Garden
Photograph by Alastair McMillan

Despite wonderful experiences in exotic locations, and many invitations, Mac has never been tempted to leave his own country permanently. Its people, its landscape and everything Irish speaks to him, providing the source of his motivation. An all green arrangement in most of his demonstrations has become his 'signature', while his favourite poet, W.B.Yeats, and the emotive works of Oscar Wilde have been a constant source of inspiration.

Quattrocento put in paint
On backgrounds for a God or Saint,
Gardens where a soul's at ease;
Where everything that meets the eye,
Flowers and grass and cloudless sky,
Resemble forms that are or seem
When sleepers wake and yet still dream,
And when they vanish still declare,
With only bed and bedstead there,
That heaven had opened...

Under Ben Bulben
W.B.Yeats

Plant Materials

Meryta sinclairii
Dypsis lutescens
Cryptocereus anthonyanus
Mandeilla amabiles
Leucadendron 'Nervosum'
Leucadendron 'Inca Gold'
Livistonia rotundifolia

Saintpaulia ionantha
bowls by Huw Powell Roberts

Corokia cotoneaster
Tulipa 'Queen of the Night'
Ophiopogon planiscapus
'Nigrescens'

Malus branches
Juniper with moss
Rhododendron macrosepalum
linearifolium

Sarracenia x courtii 'Paradisia'
Sarracenia x popei
Sarracenia x moorei

Anthurium 'Hocos Pocus'
Sarracenia courtii 'Paradisia'
Sarracenia x popei
Sarracenia x moorei
Sandersonia aurantiaca
Acer palmatum dissectum
Trachelium green

Delphinium
Rosa 'Eskimo'
Rosa glauca
Euonymus 'Silver Queen'
Sedum spectabile
Alchemilla mollis
Jasminium officinale

Trifolium repens 'William'
Lonicera periclymenum
'Serotina'

Erynigium alpinum green
Dianthus 'Barbatus'
Trachelium green
Papaver somniferum

Lathyrus 'Misty Purple'
Lathyrus 'Misty Maroon'
Rosa glauca
Heuchera 'Plum Pudding'
Pittosporum 'Irene Patterson'
Hosta 'Moonlight Sonata'

Cetaria islandica
Birch twigs
Dendranthema 'Vyking'

Corokia cotoneaster

Corokia virgata 'Bronze King'
Sarracenia x courtii 'Paradisia'

Anthurium crystallinum
Dianthus 'Barbatus'

Fagus sylvatica aurea pendula
Crocosmia
Trachelium green
Pennisetum
Hypericum
Sandersonia aurantiaca
Kniphofia
Celosia

Aspidistra elatior
Gerbera 'Hocos Pocus'

Malus branches, painted
Embothrium coccineum
Fritillaria Imperialis
Nepenthes 'Miranda'

Anthurium 'Hocos Pocus'
Acer palmatum dissectum
atropurpureum

Anthurium 'Terra'
'Green Tiger' British tomatoes
Begonia Rex

flowers, fruit and moss in variety

Protea 'Niobe'
Salix

Arachnis hybrid Orchids
Cocos nucifera
Heliconia
Ginger

Zingiber spectabile 'Shampoo'
Heliconia
Anthurium 'Tropic Night'
Anthurium 'Hocus Pocus'
Washingtonia robusta
Cordyline fruiticosa 'Black Magic'
Dracena fragrans
Leucadendron 'Safari Sunset'

Preserved Magnolia leaves
Calocedrus
Chamaecyparis

Banksia 'Hookerina'
Platycerium bifurcatum

Allium sphaerocephalon
Heuchera 'Plum Pudding'
Salix

Leucospermum
Washingtonia robusta

Sphagnum cladonia rangiferina
Sphagnum selaginella mortensii

94

Cotinus coggygria
Sphagnum cladonia rangiferina
Sphagnum selaginella mortensii
Leucobryum glaucum
Peat
Lonicera periclymenum Serotina
Prostanthera ovalifolia
Trachelium green
Astrantia major 'Roma'
Bouvardia
Trifolium
Acer palmatum atropurpureum
Eryngium

Peat
Fir
Trachelium 'Nerii Blue'
Trachelium 'Midnight'

Zantedeschia 'Mozart'
Cupressus

Bahunia spp
Pennisetum sp

Clematis 'Blue Light'

Dried palm leaves
Sunflower seeds

Platycerium bifurcatu